MW00723562

Special thanks to Griet and Ann for their friendship and support while making this book and for the transformational and powerful inner healing I have experienced at the labyrinth in lasendacostarica.com

Text copyright © 2019
Carmen Martínez Jover
www.carmenmartinezjover.com
Illustrations copyright © August 2020
Carmen Martínez Jover

Soul's Time to be Born,
an adoption story for boys
ISBN-978-607-29-2258-7

Story & Illustrations:
Carmen Martínez Jover
Layout & text layout:
Victor Nieto
flippon@gmail.com

All rights reserved.
This book may not be reproduced,
in whole nor parts, including illustrations,
in any form, without written permission
from the author.

Nicole
I dedicate this story to you.

Thank you for choosing to be in my
world and walking alongside me through the
challenges that life presents us.
I am so proud of you and grateful to have
you in my life. Travelling and creating this
book together with you, Nicole, has been
the most blissful experience ever!

I love you so much!
Mum

Soul's Time to be Born

Written and Illustrated by Carmen Martinez Jover

Luca was a beautiful soul and lived very happily in the spirit realm.

Connected to source, feeling peaceful, grateful and surrounded by unconditional love.

There he gathered with his soul group. Some had been with him before and others were ready to accompany him in the future. Some had even agreed to help through the ups and downs of life.

Luca's time had come to be born, so he went to visit the Elders and together they helped plan his new life.

The time was perfect, and the Elders gave him some important advice before he left.

The Elders said...

"Luca, when you are born remember to: be happy, love nature, be grateful, meditate, live the present moment, love and be loved, smile, be spiritual, laugh, dream, be fearless, have fun, forgive, connect, listen, care for others, be yourself, be kind."

He could have been born in many

Luca was then taken to see several life options.

different countries, had different religions and could have even been a boy or girl.

In those options,
Luca saw
Didi and Canik
for the first time.

He saw flashes of
what his life would be
with them as his Parents,
one full of adventure
and challenges, days of
laughter and also
some tears, but always
filled with lots of love.

The life he chose started with quite a challenge.

Luca was explained how he couldn't be born in a conventional way, so he'd need to find another lady's tummy in which to be born. Once born, he'd be able to make his way to his chosen parents with the help of adoption.

So, Luca accepted the challenge.

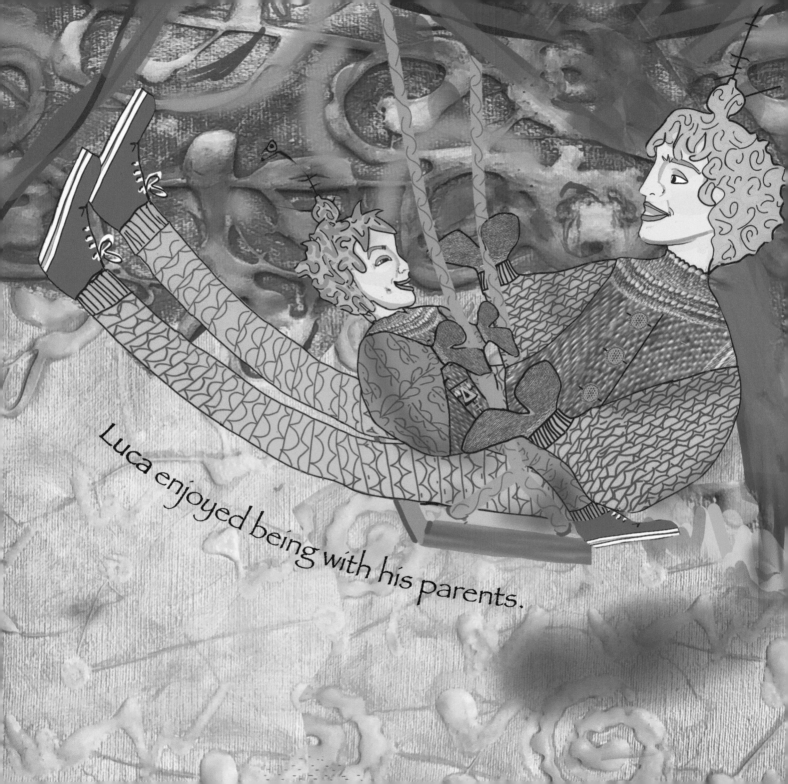

Luca enjoyed being with his parents.

Luca grew... and grew... and grew... and grew...

and lived happily facing the ups and downs of life, surrounded by his parents and friends.

Remember

what the Elder's said.

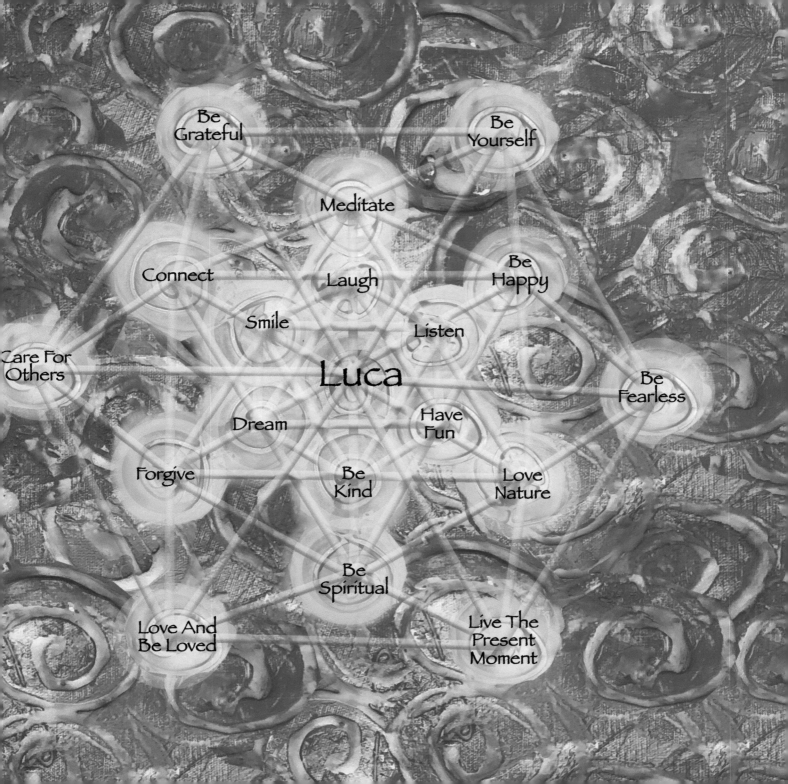

1 **Sit** down and make yourself comfortable.

2 **Close** your eyes and take **3** deep breaths.

3 **Listen to your heartbeat.**

Relax.

4 **Smile.** Feel it in your heart.

5 **Remember** and visualise **10** things you are grateful for.

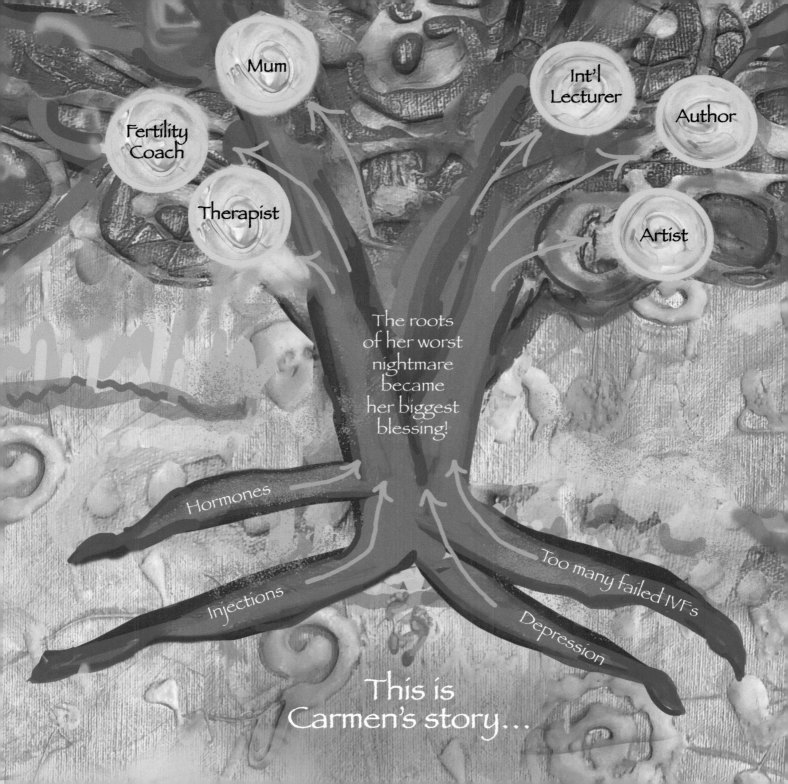

Personalise Your Own Book
books.carmenmartinezjover.com

Two Dads

I Want To Have a Child

Egg Donaton

Recipes of How Babies are Made

Adoption

Single Mum by Choice

*Available in: English, Español, Français, Italiano, русский, Português, Polsku, & Deutsch

CPSIA information can be obtained
at www.ICGtesting.com
Printed in the USA
LVHW070253080122
708047LV00002B/83

9 786072 922587